SAGRADA FAM

Helen Anderson

Published by Nine Pens Press

2022

www.ninepens.co.uk

ISBN: 978-1-7398274-9-6

015

For Georgina and Paul

Seasoned

The anniversaries are upon me:
his late-August ailments, his sudden September death,
her last, hopeless scan the day before her half-term hospital birthday,
her Halloween ambulance home, her final fading under firework sky.
Our November wedding day comes with no pearl to top our silver.
Even the good times are prefaced with wistful/regretful/raging
'would/could/should have been.'

My grandma was a shadowy widow,
keeping pointless tallies of phantom milestones.
Now, I feel her need to remember - to have people be reminded.
My husband. My daughter. Would/could/*should* have been.
The world hurtles across the seasons, regardless and shameless.
I wanted to stay with summer but the cold has been creeping in.
Cardi-weather is here.

I clutch it around me, carrying it,
never quite right. The heavy coat is coming.
I squirrel away drabs of warmth with each sly shift of the sun's angle.
I burn. I am glad, because people say pain means love.
I am supposed to post positive pictures of cosy things.
I am supposed to accept this
dreary dimming-down.

I am supposed to
write exact haikus about
tumbling, orange leaves.

The truth is my rambling terror of the trees staying bare.
That can happen, you know. I know. Here I am, my colours
out-of-kilter, all stark black frames and white screens.

Here you find me, all sock-seam blisters, dazzled by darkness-dread.
I want to have faith in the future but I am caught
up in conditional past – unreal, counterfactual, perfect.

Modals of lost opportunities bear witness
where simple tenses cannot suffice. My husband. My daughter.
Like Grandma, I will insist on reminiscence, no matter
who is not listening. This season is upon me.
Would/could/*should* have been. I am adding
real numbers. I am making our ghost stories count.

We Do Not Believe in Signs

After we viewed your body,
it was dark.
We expected rain
but stripes of light
forced through –
too faint to feel on our faces
but enough to excite our eyes.

Even if that was not you,
we knew
we were on the brink
of something bigger.
It helped
to feel
helpless and small.

There was comfort
in surrendering
to that sky.

Closing Night

There was a late show of fire,
dimmed, doused and blotted -
a hollow finale, with no audience
sing-alonging or bopping

as the credits rolled. Only
a kind tap on my elbow
indicated it was over and
wordlessly ushered me out.

"Night-night, sweetheart."
We were way beyond sleep
in that freshly vacated space.
I would not voice "goodbye."

You expect a climactic chorus
to deliver a courtesy-caution,
or at least a smouldering fade
to ease you back into yourself.

Bedside Manners

His nurse was a friend of a friend. You were not to worry.
She would be back in five to outline the plan.
They dealt with hearts like your hubby's all the time.
You perched on his bed and patted his hand, like a coper.
He said "Don't visit every day" but you had already filled out
Patient Services' form for three months' discounted parking.
He pulled his hand away, quite rudely, and nipped his nose.
He was always such a kidder. You tried to work out the joke.

He grabbed at the hospital air between you. His specs
floated to the streaky floor of his individual room.
His words came, warped and slow. "It's a stroke."
You interrupted the nurses' cuppas.
"Something's wrong." Urgent. Urgent. "Really wrong."
He was mouthing now. O-O-O-O. He meant "Stroke."
"If it is, then we'll get through it." Bright and breezy. Super-trooper.
You said it to say the right thing. You found yourself meaning it.

"We have survived worse things."
Your friend's friend shone a light in your husband's eyes.
Shadows. Glances. "Not what we want to see."
They had him sent for a scan. They had you make some calls.
No panic. Calm. Come quick.
You should have questioned the question marks
in the new doctor's eyes as she had bitten her pen
and puzzled over her doses.

You were shown to the Family Room. You were given
your own student nurse, which was not a good sign.
Your husband's cardiologist was better at bad news
than your daughter's oncologist. Soft eyes.

"A bleed, not a clot." Hard facts. "Catastrophic."
You were glad the "I love you"s had come easily, lately.
Your son, though, three hours away. "He should hurry."
You asked pertinent questions because you were an old hand.

You wish you hadn't stopped off at the Volunteer Café
after Patient Services, although, in fairness, that cheese scone
was extremely tasty and the filter coffee did keep you going
all night, topped up with tea and toast.

You wish your last text message was not about him finally
fancying half an egg sandwich, and you calling him "Fatty."
You were just kidding, too, of course, but it doesn't seem nice
or romantic, in retrospect.

Ruckus

How must it feel to roar for the sake of it
like this furious northern sea?
In darkness, I hum to the tune of the tide -
tap restless legs to its beat
from my over-sized, shoreside bed.
By day, I catch and gut stray sounds -
leave them tangled like unwound cassettes
in the blades of distant turbines.

How must it feel to yell for the thrill of it
like this jagged northern sea?
My daytime words whip away like mists
of sand storming across shingle.
All my noise has been cancelled:
I have numbed myself dumb.
How must it feel to screech like a gull -
to crash like a winter wave -

until the tide turns?

Lindisfarne Flotsam

Washed up
on Holy Island, a fragment
of kiln-fired clay. I keep coming
back to its shape: the kind of house
a child chalks. Pointy roof, wonky walls,
wavy floor. I sift the gusting sand for
chimney, windows, door. I scour the
shifting bay for a suitable shell to turn
into the girl who lives in there.

Tender Places

She possesses no vocabulary for this pain she feels.
It's "not an ache", "not a throb" – "more of a strain", she feels.

"Certainly not psychosomatic." She rubs at imperceptible
ulcers on her shin, like a baked-on stain. It feels

like she's losing whatever "it" might have been.
Yet taking tablets goes against her grain. She feels

things were best when things were left unsaid -
lips stiff and chins up. No bones about the disdain she feels

for this limp modern language of disease. No sense –
no relief for you, daughter – in urging her to explain how she feels.

Big Bed

I wish
night would come
real dark
not streetlight gloam
the house is hushed
I remember
listening for splutters
not knowing how
I would know
the sound
when it came
calling the nurse
from her bed
not wanting
to make a fuss
causing a right rumpus
my child MY CHILD
your face
pale as moon
your face
yellow like sun
holding the phone
your mouth
On Her Way
no Braxton-Hicks rattle
they wheeled you
away
by candlelight
I wish
I had made them
let me keep you

I remember
they told me straight
your dad would die
by morning
no Wait and See
dimming the switch
scraping my skull
for unsaid things
promising to try
not telling them
straight away
he had gone
knowing the sound
this time
when it came
knowing
to take my time
I think
starfish-stranded
my bed is too big
Grandma died
in bed
peaceful
they say that
I think
tea and toast
grey red-tape
unfinished fixing
I imagine
those creaks are
sleepovers
I imagine
this weight is

not hollow-fibre
I hear
the night-shift
thunk
home
for Christ's sake
now bloody birds
the day is coming
purple and green
never real
dark

Counsel

You have trained for years to remain unmoved
Your expression cannot be punctured by any admission
You peel off layers of cardigan but never reach skin
You want to know whether the tears have come yet

You make a note on your form without looking down
You will keep it in a cabinet locked with a common key
You won't tell a soul a thing, you tell me, unless
you are obliged, professionally.

You pretend not to be disappointed
Your eyes betray you by flitting to the clock
Your thoughts shift to lasagne – bubbling by now
Your calf-muscles twitch against your cable-knit skin

You want to know whether the words have come back yet
Your toenails tap in the caps of your sturdy shoes
You nod as if you know loss, too
You don't tell.

Old for New

It was that phase where we were all about vintage,
mooching around village halls at weekends,
holding ourselves and each other up and together.
You liked to consider the possibilities of stripping it all back.
I was missing pretty things.
We walked a messy line
between conserving and consuming the past
We were saviours of sad stall-holders,
buying back mismatched stuff we'd told our mothers to bin -
trying to decode makers' marks and signs of age.

It was about the hunt, for us,
and then there was the music and bunting and cake.
When we laid out our haul back home,
even the horrors were hilarious.
We found that the crazing could be the best part.
At the start, there was always spare space
yet nothing seemed to fit in.
In the end, we invented a rule
to have a place in mind before doing any deal.
By the end, we really were strict with ourselves

and each other but the garage piled itself high
with mottled mirrors and deconstructed chaises longues
and I can't get in to read the meters or get out the mower.
Every summer since, I have promised our son
I'll hire a skip or have a drive-sale or
simply give it all away.

Spelk

At the crossroads,
CACTUS FRUIT GOOD PRICE
Pedro pick out
prickles.
I take it -
tear at its topless, tailless,
flesh. Skinned,
I say *it's*
like kiwi/melon/
dragonfruit
smacking of bland
like snake.

It is and it isn't
delicious,
I say, and select
dos mas.
Quite the linguist,
sojourning at the *finca,*
punctured
by unseen barbs.
Quite the scar
seeding, to scratch at
once I seem
safely home.

Sagrada Familia (Unfinished)

Above kaleidoscope splinters,
the exact, soft shade
of Catalonian rays seeping
through sallow panes,
weeping on worshippers
crammed in the crypt below.

This holy yellow,
like mustard lamplighter daubs
on drizzling skies.
Like old-school cures for spots.
Like dandelion petals' blood,
it flecks their craned, creased necks.

Do you like butter?
Do you wet the bed?

This sacred ochre,
like shiny wrappers
untwisted from syrupy bottles
of stories of her sickness.
Like the slosh of antiseptic
on her pre-op pelvis,

a bone-white flash,
disappeared.

No time to light a candle
for all her mislaid souls,
she plunges into shadows
of plump snapdragon spires
soaring towards the palest
suggestion of summer.

Outrageous Light

This unearthly time of morning
makes me remember.
It holds me, tourniquet-tight.
This dim-dark time of morning
may as well be night:
no Nordic word for Cosy
salves the bite
of Gone is Gone.

On the marble mantel,
colourless condolences –
and a newborn baby's parents'
Thank You for the Gift.

Next Best Thing

I think about you indecently often
I like the way you cradle me
You are soft enough
They say I am too attached to you
You are hard enough
I chose you over all the others
You give me space to shove all my stuff
You know about the self-pity
You are double
You are just right
You have seen the ugly other-envy
Yet you mould to my shape
I am single again
I cannot fill you
You don't spill my secrets
You are answer enough, for now
I would pick you again
You are too young to remember
I have made you
I am lying in you

Two Years Older

(after 'Twenty-Six' by Demi Anter)

And now I am in a room of my own
Frizzing in the fret
Inking green on crumpled cream pages
I am singing with my choir

And now I am reading whole chapters
Settling the bill
Barefoot on cool tiles
I cannot pinpoint the ache

And now I am avoiding droplets
Ordering swatches for serviceable sofas
Timing gaps between waves
I am two years older than you got to be

Procession

First, the striking of the match
on a rough-sided, sulphurous box.
She waits for the wick to catch
while she slows to a stop.

As a child, she was taught to fear fire –
even flashes, even sparks,
even in Chemistry class.
As a mother, she swerved birthday cakes –
left the singeing of fingers to
others.

Now, she is aflame.

In faraway temples,
on big and small days,
tapers and tealights burn.
She watches them flicker
and soften and drip.
She sees shapes.

Restricted Palette

These times have been a smear of half-hues fashioned with make-shift tools. Christmas has been cancelled and birthdays never come. Even with faint grey graphite, I dare not dot my diary with dates.

I stay home – curtains closed - safe in monochrome. Now, my eyes have opened to winter white stripes daring me to squint at frost-feathers stippled, pink and distinct, outside. The brightness thrills me

silly and brittle-boned scared of leaving my harmless gloom and losing my grip. Stone-still on dark ice, I consider my hum drum house – fragile tongues of fake flames mirrored in plastic glass. I

consider its un-bled radiators' watery heat. I am, for a moment, convinced. I am forced bulb teased into bud. Sketch in yellow. Pale and potted beginnings of belief. For now, there is no need to know

the time of day – what week,

month, year or night it might be.

Between

I am between hills   and   sea

Family-of-four   and   lone crone

I am between unfinished book   and   learning to paint in oils

Dressing-gown   and   dressed up

I am between reunion   and   letting go

Having no space   and   time running out

I am between being wife   and   widow   and   self

Weeping wound   and   nerveless callous

I am between dusk   and   drawn curtains

Pansies   and   hyacinths

I am between dream   and   terrors

Busy-busy-busy   and   please, just stop

Midwinter

(after 'In the Bleak Midwinter' by Christina Rosetti)

There is no word
for the kind of snow
fallen this winter.
Loss frozen on loss.
Small, now, family
knots most tightly
when weather does
its worst.

You still have your
mother's love
in the shape of
the star she gave
when baubles were too bright.
You still have a
mother's love
for the child

you have
and the child
you had.
Stop making moan.
You can hear
thaw drifting
if you are
silent enough.

Stop digging out
with useless spoons.

Hunker down.
Spring will come
like Christmas
Leave that star up
all year round.
You still have

love.

How to Grow a Widow

That widow worries
a smile will start rumours she never loved him.
That widow is thankful
for the life insurance but is not feeling 'merry'.
That widow is suddenly that single-mother
of a broken, grown child.
That widow billows,
shapeless, in her time-warp shrine.

That widow dreams
he has 'only' left her for the woman next door.
That widow stuffs
her diary with purpose until she makes herself sick.
That widow is dizzy
with to-do lists, instead of poems.
That widow is on the hunt
for words vast and exact enough.

This widow ditches
her Big Girl Pants at night.
This widow suffers
fewer fools by the day.
This widow wants to shop for
flowers, not weeds.
This widow says 'no'
to silence and shadow.

This widow has shifted,
slow and out of sight,
from 'What would he have done?'
to 'I am doing this.'

This widow mourns, though.
This widow misses.

ACKNOWLEDGEMENTS

'We Do Not Believe in Signs' was first published on Twitter by Imperial Spark on 1 July 2020

'Tender Places' was first published by *Fragmented Voices* on 25 March 2020

'Ruckus' was first published as 'Rumpus' in the 'Hard Times Happen' anthology (Black Pear Press, 2021)

'Big Bed' was first published on Carmen Marcus' blog *The Book of Godless Verse* on 2 November 2019

'*Sagrada Familia* (Unfinished)' was first published in *Anthology 1. Light* (The Black Light Engine Room Press, 2020)

'Outrageous Light' was first published as part of *Celebrating Change*: *Trauma series* on 24 April 2020

'How to Grow a Widow' was *Diamond Twig Poem of the Month* in July 2020

Lightning Source UK Ltd.
Milton Keynes UK
UKHW041923041222
413331UK00005B/161